I0832857

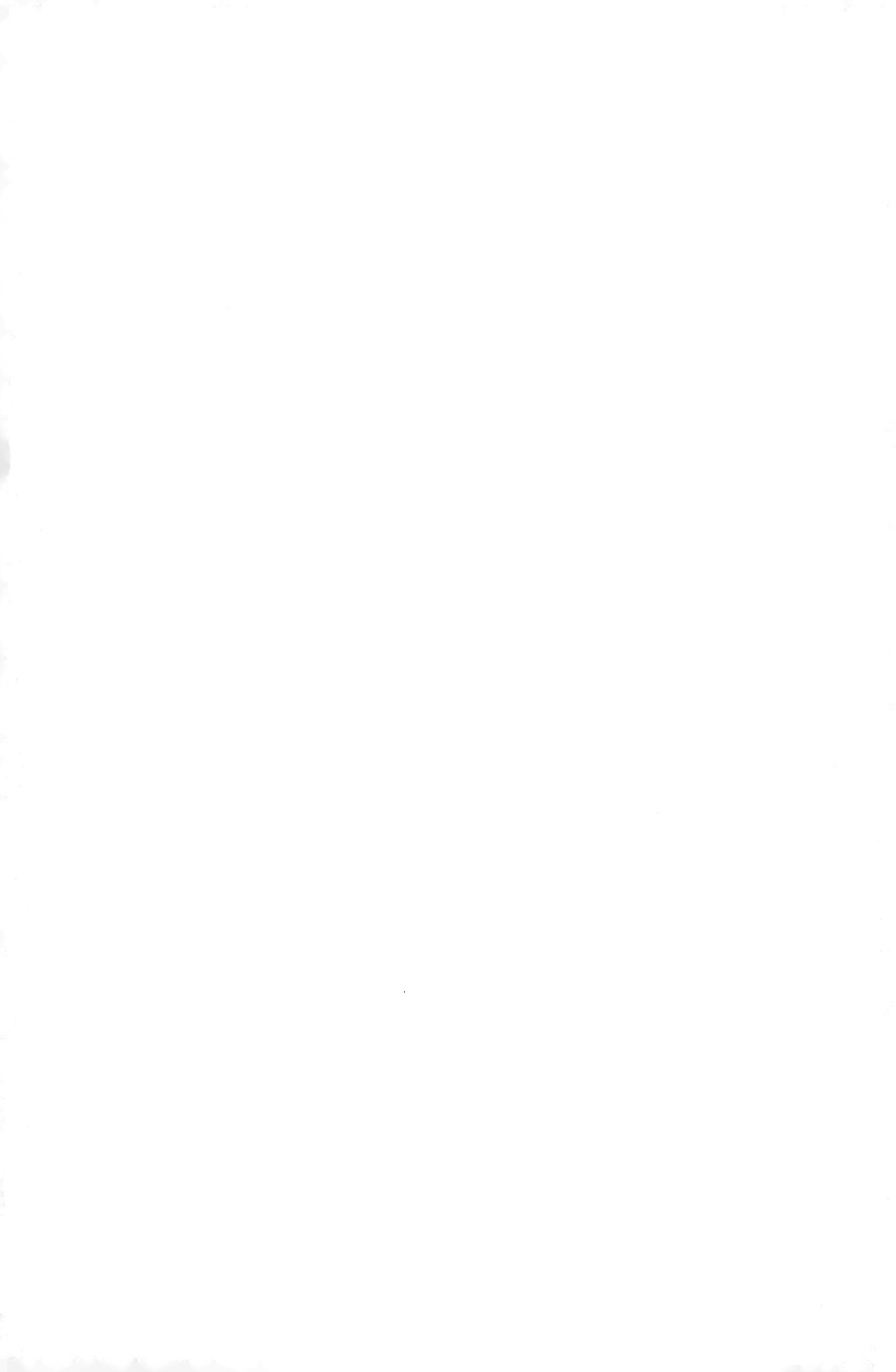

A Song in the Timing I Needed

-Volume 1-

A Song in the Timing I Needed

Volume 1

Owen Watson, Ph.D.

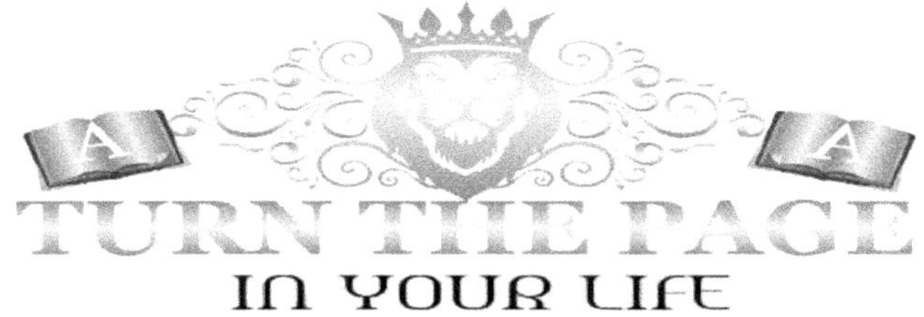

A Song in the Timing I Needed
Volume 1

Copyright © 2024 by Owen Watson, Ph.D.

All rights reserved. No part of this book may be used or reproduced in any manner whatsoever without written permission except in the case of brief quotations embodied in critical articles and reviews. For more information, Email drowenwatson@outlook.com

Author Owen Watson's books may be purchased for educational, business, or sales promotional use. For information, visit www.drowenwatson.com

First Edition

Cover Design By: Owen Watson, Ph.D.

Editor: Ramona L. Watson, Ph.D.

Library of Congress Cataloging-in-Publication Data

ISBN-978-1-957420-08-0

Dedication

To those who continuously carry a tune of thankfulness in their hearts in spite of. Although people, circumstances, and life aren't always what you expected, you have encouragingly impacted people, circumstances, and other lives in the world around you. You have been the words seamlessly fitted into their life melodies that have produced timeless songs of inspiration. May time with God continue being your priority as you go about sharing His song of love, hope, and peace by serving others to His glory.

Contents

Introduction

Whether in difficult or delightful times, each of us seems to find a tune that either inspires or empowers us. It may be something we've heard and know well [word for word]; it may be an instrumental melody of some sort [that we improvise with our own lyrics]; or it may be altogether a spontaneous naturally created melody with lyrics of our own. Whatever and however the inspiring or empowering tune emerges, it holds our attention as being the right song at the right time. That is the basis of this book, *A Song in the Timing I Needed.*

A Song in the Timing I Needed seeks to link the personalized imagined melodies we find ourselves humming audibly or in our thoughts (as we go about our days whether in chaos or at peace) with corresponding affirmative lyrics that shine the light on God's goodness. Since we are regarded as new creations in Christ (according to 2 Corinthians 5:17), the beauty of singing new songs is understanding the innate joy of God at work in and through our lives. Experiencing such joy translates to appreciative expressions through psalms and hymns as spoken in Ephesians 5:19, "...speaking to one another in psalms and hymns and spiritual songs, singing and making melody in your heart to the Lord..." As your tunes are accompanied by the lyrics within this book your soul will surely be revived, the eyes of your heart opened, and life perspectives will yield to God being seen as the priority.

Above It All

The lyrics of *Above It All* are set to a slow tempo tune for worship. They focus on reflections and appreciating the mightiness of God as He is high above everything imaginable and beyond. The lyrics follow a genesis pattern, recognizing creation from the beginning of time to our present day experiences. They intentionally offer warm expressions of solace and gratefulness for God's omnipotence and omnipresence, reassuring our hearts with the knowledge and understanding (without a shadow of doubt) that no matter what we're going through God stands immovably above it all. No matter what we're going through, no matter how detrimentally dire situations and circumstances may be, God's above it all! No matter what season of life we're facing, God's above it all! God continually comforts, protects, strengthens, and guides us above it all!

Knowing that God resides among us should be more than enough reason for us to stand tall and walk boldly amid an iniquitous world. Just go outside and look up into the sky. He created and is above it all! Take a moment to imagine how grand God is! Guess what? He's above anything you could ever imagine! As far as we can see naturally in any direction, whether our crippling circumstances are small or large, God is above it all! As sure as He is above it all, He is also capable of performing a paradigm shift for all things to work for our good!

Think on that time when it seemed as though everything and everyone was against you, and you felt alone and very overwhelmed. Not knowing how you were going to escape or where or who you could turn to, you surrendered in prayer and realized He was and is above it all. Suddenly, you were brought to your spiritual sense of security in Him which inspired and guided you through. His peace didn't come by the circumstances changing, it came by you releasing those issues which were stealing your joy and blocking you from seeing Him and His glory. The moment you sincerely gave them to Him, your eyes were opened to see Him and receive His peace. That's the benefit of seeing Him above it all!

He provides us His Holy Spirit, a piece of Him, that enables us to soar above the troubles in which we may find ourselves. He loves us so much that He's ever with us and among us! He's the gentleness of the calm winds and the strength of the most powerful winds! When you think of creation, recognize that He created all things. Notwithstanding, this song is penned to make you ponder and give thanks for the greatness of God in every aspect of who He is and how all is under His control!

Above It All (lyrics)

(*worship – slow tempo*)

The heavens and the earth
Galaxies throughout all of space
The entire universe

Above it all is the Most High

The sun, moon, and stars
Changes of seasons for various reasons
Everything near and afar

Above it all is the Most High

Every created being
Established powers and positions
Everything we're seeing

Above it all is the Most High

Unbearable circumstances
People who are unkind
Failures resulting from chances

Above it all is the Most High
Above it all is the Most High…

You are Creator [of everything]
You are Arranger [of everything]

You are Healer [of everything]
You are Changer [of everything]
Everything answers to You [the Creator}
Everything is set by You [the Arranger]
Everything can be made whole [the Healer]
Everything can be turned around [the Changer]

You are God!
You are God!
And You're above it all…!
Yes, You are God!
You are God!
And You're above it all…!

There's nothing nor no one higher
Within us You the spark the burning fire
We thank You for our heart's desire
to worship You above it all…

You are Creator [of everything]
You are Arranger [of everything]
You are Healer [of everything]
You are Changer [of everything]
Everything answers to You [the Creator}
Everything is set by You [the Arranger]
Everything can be made whole [the Healer]
Everything can be improved [the Changer]

You are God!
You are God!
And You're above it all…!
Yes, You are God!
You are God!
And You're above it all…!

Hallelujah…
We lift our voices

Hallelujah…
We lift our hands
Hallelujah…
We bow before You
Hallelujah…
On Your word we stand

You are Creator [of everything]
You are Arranger [of everything]
You are Healer [of everything]
You are Changer [of everything]
Everything answers to You [the Creator}
Everything is set by You [the Arranger]
Everything can be made whole [the Healer]
Everything can be improved [the Changer]

You are God!
You are God!
And You're above it all…!
Yes, You are God!
You are God!
And You're above it all…!

Hallelujah,
You're above it all…!

Back on the Stand Again

Back on the Stand Again is a solemn song which opens with us taking a circumspect view of how others, the enemy (Satan), or even we condemn ourselves to the depths of feeling of little worth and/or living subpar lives. After all, scripture holds that we are born in sin [i.e., wickedness, flawed, etc.] and prone to going in the ways of sin (Psalm 51:5). In a nutshell, sin is what we know and how we live apart from God. What Satan does is use sin to fuel his cases, brought before God, against you and me. He continually takes these cases before God to condemn us, and He replays them in our minds to discredit God's acceptance of us. It's a repetitive theme of his [Satan] – to sow discord and doubt between God and mankind. He's a killer of righteous relationships. Even in our running, the enemy steadily plants and waters the seed that leads to us being on the stand alone and inexperienced in defending ourselves. Sadly, many of us fall for the bait and choose to conceal sins and go about our comfortably condemned ways rather than disclosing sins, repenting, and accepting the true love of God in Christ.

But the song goes on to provide an answer of truth and encouragement! It awakens us to the knowledge of us being children of a loving and forgiving God, the ultimate sacrifice made for us being reconciled to God, and the greatest and only defense attorney – JESUS – who guarantees us an exoneration from Satan's charges. When we pray and go to God carrying burdens of guilt, we must not grieve the Holy Spirit within us by doubting and feeling unworthy. The Holy Spirit gives us boldness, assures us of victory by Jesus' resurrection, and seeks to guide us in righteousness by the Word of God [i.e., the Bible] that has been provided to us! Whenever we're found *Back on the Stand Again*, we must know who's representing us and allow the Holy Spirit to lessen those court appearances by perfecting us in Christ.

Back on the Stand Again (lyrics)

(*slow tempo*)

Finding myself being where I've been before
after promising myself to close that door
Now I'm back trapped in the prison of sin
while being condemned back on the stand again
I prayed so hard to keep from falling
but the temptation got the win
I need expedited help without stalling
to keep from getting back on the stand again

Life's a difficult road to travel
trying to live each day as one should
Loving my neighbors as I love myself
and treating everyone with kindness, just being good

However, when I get with wrong crowds
and try so hard to fit in to their mold
I sacrifice my moral compass
in exchange for their approval

Forgetting who I am in Christ,
I do what I know I shouldn't do
That's why I'm on my knees
asking forgiveness and crying out to You

Finding myself being where I've been before
after promising myself to close that door
Now I'm back trapped in the prison of sin
while being condemned back on the stand again
I prayed so hard to keep from falling
but the temptation got the win
I need expedited help without stalling
to keep from getting back on the stand again

One day I heard a voice
still but strongly whispering in the wind
saying, "Son, your sins have been forgiven long ago"
At that moment, my eyes were opened wide
and a calmness comforted my soul
as joyful tears started to flow

For there were many times
when I presumed God disowned me
due to my falling into continual sin
Condemnation had a grip on me
making me think I'll always lose and never win
But with God as the Judge and Christ my defense
I was guaranteed mercy in the end
whenever I found myself back on the stand again

Finding myself being where I've been before
after promising myself to close that door
now I'm back trapped in the prison of sin
while being condemned back on the stand again
Thank God that my prayers have been answered
knowing that His death on the cross defeated sin
I now cling to faith that is no longer tampered
as I go boldly and ready to get back on the stand again

Cathartic

If you're seeking earnest expressions of worship, *Cathartic* should be that song. The lyrics are rooted in seeing and trusting God personally as your reason and source for everything possible and impossible. Coupled with a slow tempo tune, it will transport you to a place of tearful worship! It undresses and draws out your heart's most passionate and sincere emotions, representing all of you, and willfully delivers utmost reverence to God. The song embodies believing and trusting God, taking Him at His word – reminding us that as we follow after Him, we're accepting more of Him by surrendering to Him. It frees His Holy Spirit for doing a work within us and bringing us into His presence.

Thinking back, when was the last time you opened your heart to God? I mean really and truly opened your heart to Him beyond wanting material things? Here's one for you - When is the last time you spontaneously sought and appreciated Him for who He is? When our eyes are open to seeking more of His face than His hand, we become less images of ourselves and greater reflections of Jesus. There is something that really ignites within us when we have those one-on-one moments of intimate expressions with Him.

Cathartic is a worship song that encourages us to praise God in spite of. It's a pouring out of the heart to say, "God I'm accepting more of you, I'm believing more of you, I'm trusting more of you, I'm living more for you." It'll ready you to live a life that's driven, that shines, and that is on fire for sharing His goodness with others.

Cathartic (lyrics)

(*worship – slow tempo*)

Praising You in the midst of
all that's going on around,
loving You when there is no love
in this world found;
Seeking You as a confidant
and a friend,
knowing You could do
what no one else can

You are my reason
for this song I sing
You are my cry
a cathartic release of everything

Asking You
to give what no one else can
Honoring Your word
as best I can;
Wanting You always
in my life forever
Greater You are
forever

You are my reason
for this song I sing
You are my cry
a cathartic release of everything

I am whole
I am new
I am blessed
I know You as truth
I am standing
I am stable
I am strong
I am able
I am complete
I am at peace
I am inspired
I am free

You are my reason
for this song I sing
You are my cry
a cathartic release of everything

[*repeat entire song twice*]

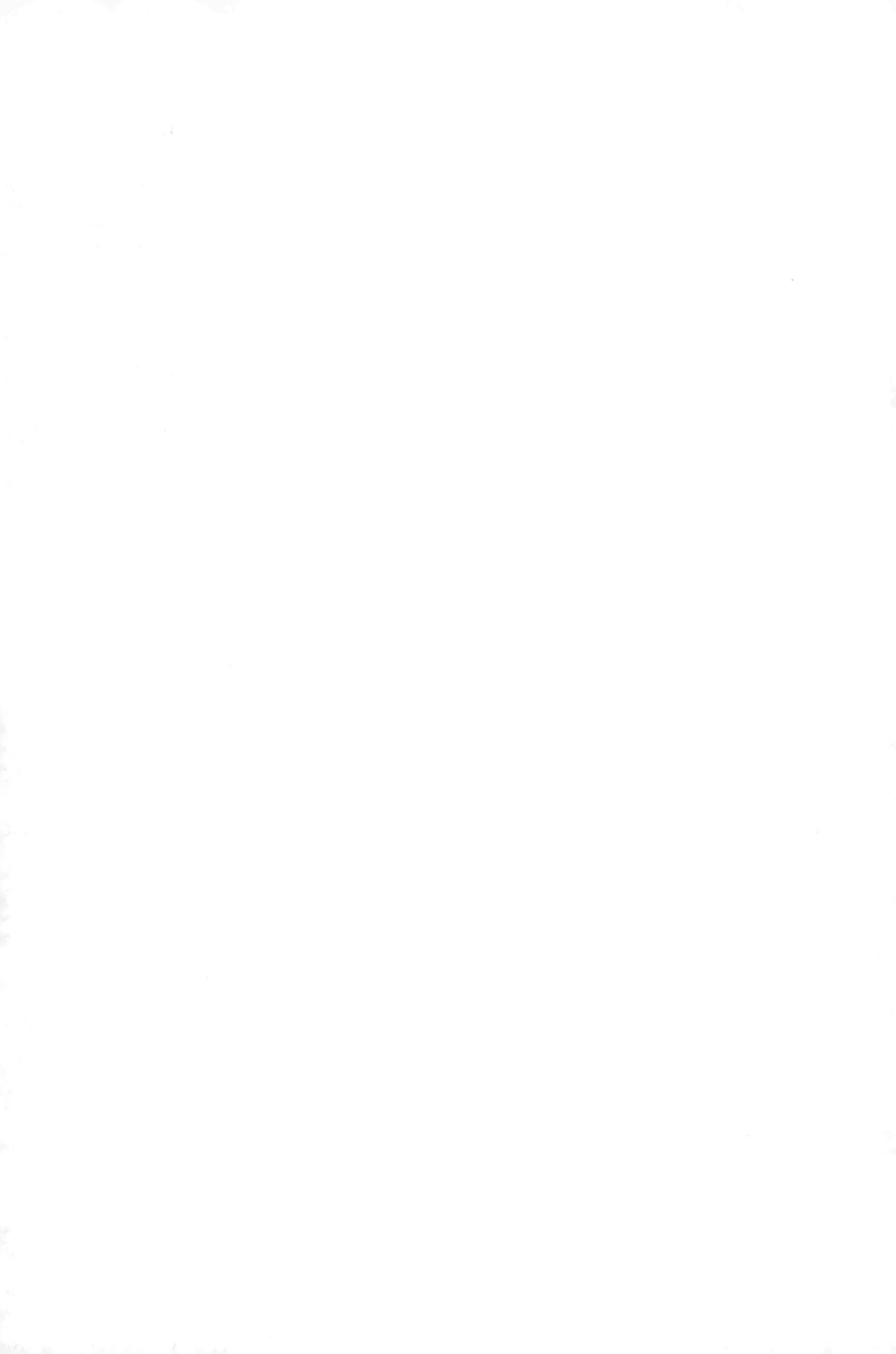

Deeper

Deeper is a song that embodies being content with God in all things. The lyrics are intended to accompany stanzas that are slow in tempo and gradually climax into a high energy, up-tempo chorus. The lyrical scheme is to place you one-on-one in the presence of God while simultaneously challenging you to go deeper in prayer, worship, and revelation of Him. Suddenly, as you find yourself submerged in Him, you can prophetically see yourself going deeper in living life in honor of Him, going deeper in praising Him, having a deeper appetite for reading the Bible, as well as going deeper in having things revealed to you by Him. This all culminates in having an intimately personal relationship with Him like no other in comparison. This type of relationship fully equips you for carrying out His calling and ordained purpose for you.

Without a doubt, oftentimes when we experience troubling times in our lives, most of us habitually turn to God as a last resort. While it is good that we do know who to turn to [God], it would be much better if He is the priority rather than last option. When we have a lifestyle that puts Him first, not only do we gain knowledge, but we also gain godly wisdom for either avoiding hardships altogether or boldly, peacefully, and safely maneuvering through them. We make Him first by fostering a deeper and sustainable genuine relationship with Him.

In essence, *Deeper* is a song of willfully and truly embracing God as your everything. Each stanza is a proclamation of surrender to Him and dependency on Him. The story being relayed is that of a personal acceptance of Him as your need. It's a song of answering His calling by way of committedly worshipping Him!

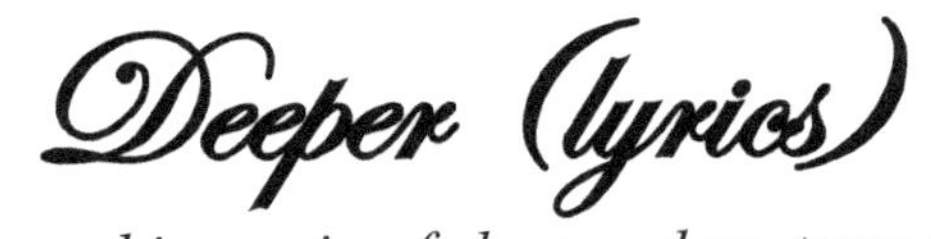

(worship – mix of slow and up-tempo)

Deeper in love with You,
that's where I'm falling

Everyday that You catch me
I become confident more and more

Deeper in love with You,
that's how I'm living

Everyday as I trust in Your word
I am changed from the core

Deeper in love with You,
that's how I'm building

Everyday that I stand on what You say
there's nothing I can't do

Deeper in love with You,
that's why I'm adjusting

Everyday as I live this life
I am made brand new

Deeper and deeper
I find myself wrapped in You,
not caring about tomorrow
cause' I know you'll bring me through,

not sizing up what others have
but appreciating that I am Yours,
patiently waiting to enter into Your presence
behind glorious doors

Deeper in love with You,
that's why I'm serving

Everyday as I'm in the world
there's a purpose for my life

Deeper in love with You,
that's what I'm embracing

Everyday is an opportunity
for me to share Your light

Deeper in love with You,
knowing how much You love me

Everyday I'm blessed
to share and run the race

Deeper in love with You,
my soul cries out with great joy

Everyday I find peace
As I humbly kneel before Your face

Deeper and deeper
I find myself wrapped in You,
not caring about tomorrow
cause' I know you'll bring me through,
not sizing up what others have
but appreciating that I am Yours,
patiently waiting to enter into Your presence
behind glorious doors

You are unsearchable
Yet, all resides in You
You are immeasurable
Yet, You're in my heart
You are infallible
Yet, You love me too
You are my Promise
and we'll never be apart

As I go deeper and deeper
I find myself wrapped in You,
not caring about tomorrow
cause' I know you'll bring me through,
not sizing up what others have
but appreciating that I am Yours,
patiently waiting to enter into Your presence
behind glorious doors

Deeper and deeper,
I'm planting myself in You
Deeper and deeper,
I'm growing in you
Deeper and deeper,
I need more of You!

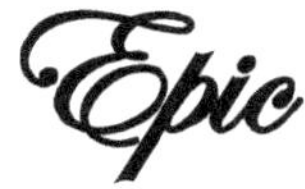

Epic is a song of gratitude to our astounding God with lyrics written to accompany a compelling slow tempo melody. It's a song meant to provoke you to take a time travel from where you were in your life to where you are with Him purposefully in your life. As you look back over snippets of your life's past, inspect the failures (God was there), inspect the struggles (God was there), inspect the "NO" answers (God was there), inspect the loneliness (God was there), and so much more – but in and through them all, God was there in an epic way! There were times when guilt made us believe we were unfit for coming to God. That was a lie! There were times when we accepted a non-existent relationship with Him. That wasn't His plan. There were times when we had given up on there being any relief in meeting specific needs in our lives. Yet, He used someone or some situation to come through right on time! Surely as He is an epic God, He does epic things on our behalf!

Let's not only look back at our lives, let's look at God's epic history. God sacrificed His only begotten son for each of us. He didn't have to, but He did! In the midst of us living in sin and rejecting Him, He patiently called us unto salvation. He didn't need to, but He so loved us! He provides His word [i.e., the Bible] for us to nurture a relationship with Him and we rarely, if ever, make time for Him. He doesn't distance Himself from us, but He bridged the gap allowing for willing access.

Epic is a song of oneness and awareness of what He has done because of His undeniable, unconditional love for us. It was an epic account for Christ to sinlessly go to the cross and be crucified for the sins of the world. For Him to go to the grave and be resurrected for the surety of our salvation was epic. He was looking out for us. All accounts in the Bible are epic because of His infinite love. He favors us with epic mercy, love, and more! This is a song that captivates your heart and soul resulting in an epic response of rejoicing.

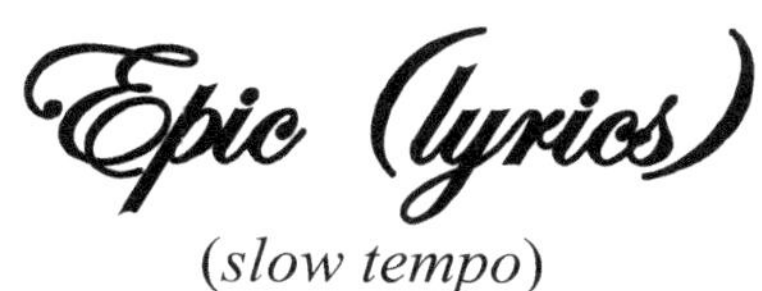

Epic (lyrics)

(*slow tempo*)

Looking back on who I was,
it was amazing that You would ever want me
Seeing who I am now,
it blows my mind how You transformed me

All that I thought was good
was only preventing me from Who is good
The good I had known blinded me
but the good of Who You are set me free

My life was on the line
as I lived selfishly for pleasure and praise
Not knowing that none of that could save me
when I'm on my death bed in the final days

Thankful I am for the life I have in You,
instantly I give You glory and praise
Steadfast ready to sing songs to You
with mouth wide-open and hands raised

I was that sinner
who should've been on that cross
I was so far out there
living to die, simply lost
Then You called out to me
through a hunger and thirst,
it all led to me falling behind

and putting You first
It was your mercy and grace
getting us connected
The testimony of Your love that saves
is nothing less than epic

To You I dedicate
each and every day
In the morning when I awaken,
it's to You whom I pray

You have that epic kind of grace
You have that epic kind of love
You provide that epic kind of washing
Which cleanses us by the blood
You are epic, God!

Living this life sharing who You are,
I am the product of Your love and mercy
Satisfied in who I am now
Jesus was the price paid for me

All that I wanted could never compare
to Who I needed
Who I needed was not what I wanted
but I'm thankful my request was superseded

I was called to something better
and to do greater in the world around
The selfish sinner me is fading away,
no longer are sin and weights holding me bound

The greatness of Your Love
freed me from the ways of society
I am now committed to You,
captured in the hands of the Almighty

I was that sinner
who should've been on that cross
I was so far out there
living to die, simply lost
Then You called out to me
through a hunger and thirst,
it all led to me falling behind
and putting You first
It was your mercy and grace
getting us connected
The testimony of Your love that saves
is nothing less than epic

To You I dedicate myself
each and every day
In the morning when I awaken,
it's to You whom I pray

You have that epic kind of grace
You have that epic kind of love
You give us that epic kind of life
You are more than enough
You make that epic kind of change
You make that epic kind of way out
You give us that epic kind of hope
You put our lives on a glorious route
You are epic, God!

Featuring the King of Kings

As Christians, the highlight of our everyday should be living a life that features Jesus! In this song, *Featuring the King of Kings*, the lyrics depict us needing, finding, and being secured in Him. The lyrics are written to produce a profound slow tempo worship song which illustrates the significance of us having a relationship with Him. It's a song about us daily waking up and not knowing what the day holds but finding security and strength in knowing Who holds the day. However, for us to attain the peace and wisdom for navigating through the days ahead and beyond the trials of yesterday, we are hard-pressed to have the King of Kings show up in and through our lives!

We can all agree that a time of progressions is time well spent. What better way to progress in a relationship with God than spending time with God? It's in the time spent pursuing Him that we learn humility, gain clarity, and develop spiritually. In doing so, we stand ready to glorify Him by introducing the King of Kings to those around us by how we treat them. We are comforted by His presence, and as the Holy Spirit is doing a work within us, we become billed cast members of God's production of, "The will of God being done on earth as it is in heaven," *Featuring the King of Kings*!

Featuring the King of Kings (lyrics)

(*worship – slow tempo*)

The day before me,
I know not what it holds

What bothered me yesterday
I must let it all go

As I awaken this morning,
my eyes must see a new thing
It has to be hope for today
featuring the King of Kings

Lord, let me have my piece of You,
strength and courage for getting me through
all the things known and what is to come

Lord, hear what I'm praying to You
and impart Your Spirit's comfort of truth,
so that I may perform what is well done

The day is hectic,
ushering in stress and fear

It's easy to lose focus
especially when I forget You're here

I take a break from the distractions
and find a comforting song to sing,
it's my rope of salvation from the madness,
featuring the King of Kings

Lord, in You I find the peace I need,
please fill me up through word and deed
that I may be prepared for the work ahead

Lord, I know You hear my cry,
Your child You will not deny
I'm standing on every word You said

With You being on the throne,
lifted high and evident in my life,
that's when I'm used by You
to bring peace and share the light

The world needs to know
and they need to see a greater thing
It all starts with introducing You by how I live
featuring the King of Kings

Jesus, Jesus
Jesus, Jesus
You are the King of Kings!

The day before me,
I know not what it holds

What bothered me yesterday
I must let it all go

The day is hectic,
ushering in stress and fear

It’s easy to lose focus
especially when I forget You’re here

The world needs to know
and they need to see a greater thing
It all starts with introducing You by how I live
featuring the King of Kings

Jesus, I surrender to You!
You are the King of Kings!
Jesus, Jesus
Jesus, Jesus
I surrender to You!
You are the King of Kings!

Gifted to Share God's Goodness

Undeserving we are, yet He loves us and gifts us with His goodness! *Gifted to Share God's Goodness* is an introspective, infectious slow tempo worship tune that is written with the intention of goading us into understanding and accepting our gifting and purpose as His children in this world. The lyrics strongly imply the knowledge of us being unqualified, yet He accepts us by grace. In His grace, He revives, sees, and positions us as qualified to share His goodness with the world around us. Upon receiving His grace, His spirit begins the operating procedure in our lives, rebuilding our foundation based on His word and ridding us of the old, futile foundation which was built on this world. Once we've been connected to Him, we're positioned to receive what nurtures and produces the fruit of the Spirit for the benefit of those around us. The nurturing comes by spending prayer time with Him, partaking of His word [i.e., reading the Bible, going to church, etc.], and sharing common life circumstances. It's by His goodness we're able to maintain godliness and selflessly withstand temptations.

In Him, we become reflections of Him, His goodness! He gifts us not for us to hoard but to share. In the essence of sharing, we're praising and worshipping Him as our lifestyle is being introduced to others who need what He only can provide [through us]. His goodness allows us the opportunity of being the light and salt this world lacks and needs. As read in the lyrics, the questions are asked, "Why me?" and "Why now?". When we understand that He is the loving, forgiving, and merciful God who calls us because He created us, we can then humbly know the answers to "Why me?" and "Why now?" It all leads back to the core of His goodness, not willing that any should perish.

Gifted to Share God's Goodness (lyrics)

(*worship – slow tempo*)

Why me?
You chose me
Why me?
Why me?
Why me?

There's nothing special about me
that sets me apart from another
Yet, You called me out
to share Your goodness with others
Unqualified and filled with shame,
guilty on every count as the enemy claims
but You provided a way for me to call Your name
and my life has never been the same
because of Your goodness

Your goodness, I will share
in how I treat my neighbor
in how I rest in Your care
in seeing You as Greater
I'm gifted to share
Your goodness,
Your goodness

Why now?
I don't feel ready
Why now?
Why now?
Why now?

With You, time is in Your hand
let the hands of the clock fall where they may
Timing is what You make it to be
which is beyond what we know as night and day
The time to move is when You speak
Oftentimes it's when we're found weak
The glory is Yours alone not for us to seek
Have Your way Lord with the meek
because of Your goodness

Your goodness, I will share
in how I treat my neighbor
in how I rest in Your care
in seeing You as Greater
I'm gifted to share
Your goodness,
Your goodness,
Your goodness,
Your goodness

Why me?
You chose me
Why now?
I don't feel ready
I have nothing of value to offer
except the emptying of who I am
You accept my emptiness
and gift me with Your goodness
to share
Your goodness, I will share!
Your goodness, I will share!

Your goodness, I will share
in how I treat my neighbor
in how I rest in Your care
in seeing You as Greater
I'm gifted to share
Your goodness,
Your goodness,
Your goodness,
Your goodness,
Your goodness,
Your goodness, I will share!

Heaven's Afterparty

Heaven's Afterparty is written as an up-tempo joyful song. It expresses the joy we're to experience together with the angels in heaven upon our being welcomed to heaven. The lyrics provide a glimpse of the glorious estate Jesus has readied for us in the presence of God. It is a home more extravagant in comparison to any building ever made on earth. We have a future among angels, loved ones who have passed before us, new introductions to those who have inspired us, and most importantly, we will be in a holistic relationship with God Himself! *Heaven's Afterparty* will be the manifested byproduct of our faith. We will be part of a nation of people who are excited about God, excited about sharing victories from the smallest to the ultimate, excited about His righteousness, and excited that we repented and accepted Him when we did! Just imagine being up there with Him, high above the universe where there's no more sin, no more sorrows, no more tears! We shall have freedom to worship, to live eternally in righteousness, to praise and worship always!

Heaven's Afterparty (lyrics)

(*up-tempo*)

There's coming a day
when we will be met by Jesus
Seeing Him face to face,
very grateful for Him saving us

At that great sound of the trumpet
all our troubles we will forget
We'll be overwhelmed by His presence
free of troubles and all sin debt

Upon arrival,
just beyond the gates,
we'll join the angels rejoicing
for something that'll be great

As we begin walking
on streets of gold,
all of heaven's hosts will proclaim aloud,

"WELCOME TO HEAVEN'S AFTERPARTY!

He's prepared this home for you
and as you can see
nothing on earth could've compared
to this destiny
No more day and night
We are all time-free

So let's enjoy what is
for all eternity"

Heaven's Afterparty
[This is Heaven's Afterparty]
Heaven's Afterparty...
[This is Heaven's Afterparty]
Heaven's Afterparty...

There we shall be reunited
with loved ones and friends,
remembering and sharing
the good times had back then

But most and best of all
is knowing we all made it in,
ready to receive rewards
straight from the King's hand

There'll be a celebration,
as we're welcomed in our mansion home,
with all of heaven's hosts proclaiming,

"WELCOME TO HEAVEN'S AFTERPARTY!

He's prepared this home for you
and as you can see
nothing on earth could've compared
to this destiny
No more day and night
We are all time-free
So let's enjoy what is
for all eternity"

Heaven's Afterparty
[This is Heaven's Afterparty]
Heaven's Afterparty...

[This is Heaven's Afterparty]
Heaven's Afterparty…
[This is Heaven's Afterparty]
Heaven's Afterparty…
[This is Heaven's Afterparty]
Heaven's Afterparty…

WELCOME HOME!

I Know You (God)

Having an unshakeable, undeniable confidence in God being God is the idea being relayed in the lyrics of *I Know You (God)*. The lyrical expressions paint a picture of various life experiences that are unable to overtake what God provides [i.e., joy, peace, memories, hope, etc.] to sustain us. His provision serves as a reminder of Him being present in all aspects of our lives no matter what. The lyrics are meant as a song of worship (slow tempo). It shares the results of grasping the knowledge and accepting Him as God despite.

If you've been walking with God and witnessed having your needs met spiritually, which cancelled out the worries you were experiencing at the time, you can relate to what is being communicated in this song. You have a testimony of the unimaginable but realistic spiritual fruits He has provided in getting you beyond places of helplessness, hopelessness, and/or homelessness. Likewise, this song encourages us to stand boldly and press forward through whatever the day brings. This song serves as a reinforcement of our faith in God. It is a personal declaration and inspiration which declares *I Know You (God)*!

I Know You (God) (lyrics)

(*worship – slow tempo*)

When life does what life does
and happens
I still have joy,
unimaginable joy

When plans fail and I'm left
without any other options
I still have peace,
unimaginable peace

When the crowd leaves
and I'm left all alone
I still have precious memories,
unimaginable precious memories

When I experience
moments of doubt
I still have hope,
unimaginable hope

When it looks like
I'm in major trouble
I still have amazing grace,
unimaginable amazing grace

When I'm feeling useless
and told I'm worthless

I still have purpose
unimaginable purpose

when I think I've
reached the end of my rope
I still have strength,
unimaginable strength

I know You (God),
You love this child of Yours
You are my everything
my unimaginable everything
Because I know You,
life is a blessing everyday
You are my song,
You're the reason I sing

I know You (God),
I know You (God),
I love You, Lord
I love You, Lord

Forever You are
and forever You will be
The universe's blessing
living in the heart of people like me
To know You
is to rest assured,
trusting You as our future
with so much more in store

I know You (God),
I love You, Lord
I know You (God),
I love You, Lord
I know You (God),
I love You, Lord

I know You (God),
I know You, You are my God!

Joining to Serve

Joining to Serve is more than a song, it is a campaign that stirs us to fulfill our Father's will by being about the kingdom business of serving. The lyrics take us on an introspective journey regarding the needs around us. They are to be complemented with a slow to mid-tempo melody that incites love in action on our part. Furthermore, the lyrics highlight our mission of serving others beyond what we see and think. It enlarges the definition of love from the confined limits of what we perceive it as being to a boundless exemplification of who and what God is.

Serving is our commissioned duty and responsibility according to the will of God. Oftentimes and sadly, we haughtily turn our noses up and delegate these duties and responsibilities to the world. In doing so, we grieve the Holy Spirit by being self-servers rather than serving others. The love of God in our lives should never be caged and utilized as a quid-pro-quo type weapon. It [God's love] is to be shared in the opportunities around us, whether it's at church, a community center, a homeless shelter, wherever.

As you're singing *Joining to Serve,* allow it to inspire you to serve others with the heart of Jesus as led by the Holy Spirit. Know that we are the contagious change that betters the world around us.

Joining to Serve (lyrics)

(slow to mid-tempo)

Wanting,
but there's nothing to be had
Living,
on the streets without a bed
Searching,
everywhere for daily bread
These are thoughts I have
about those on the streets as I observe
This is what pushes me
out of my comfort zone to serve

Saying,
I wish more could be done
Praying,
God it takes more than just one
Knowing,
for many life hasn't begun
These are thoughts I have
that breaks me from being reserved
This is what pushes me
out of my comfort zone to serve

Everyone has a story
that leads to where they are
Unfortunately, many have no glory
when darkness was their start
Who am I to be condescending,

to have what I have yet withhold giving
My attitude can't be "That's what they deserve!"
God forgive my heart and lead me to serve

Looking,
around the streets in disbelief
Needing,
a way to help provide relief
Drowning,
with a broken heart of grief
These are thoughts I have
for those on the streets as I observe
This is what pushes me
out of my comfort zone to serve

Everyone has a story
that leads to where they are
Unfortunately, many have no glory
when darkness was their start
Who am I to be condescending,
to have what I have yet withhold giving?
My attitude can't be "That's what they deserve!"
God forgive my heart and lead me to serve

We are all born into this world,
some in love and care, some without
For those who have to give,
let the serving business be what we're about
For the day will come as we stand at heaven's door
when lives will be judged based on faith and doubt
Seize the opportunity to do what can be done now,
expanding His kingdom here on earth, leaving none left out

Join to serve
Is the mission we're called to do
Join to serve
It's what Jesus did for me and you

Join to serve
Be the difference this world needs
Join to serve
Put your words into action by your deeds
Join to serve…
Join to serve…
Join to serve…!

Let's make life better
for those who are without
Let's not be the reason for
"God" to be a story doubt
Let's be about our Father's business,
not judging by what anyone deserves,
but by illustrating God's love
by joining to serve…

Keeping the Faith

Keeping the Faith is written as a soulful spiritual to be accompanied by a slow tempo melody. The lyrics center around God's faithfulness throughout our lives which has produced and continues to produce testimonies of Him being there with us through the good, the bad, and everything in between. It is a song written to encourage the soul as we continue to keep the faith and not lose track of His presence.

When reading the lyrics and setting it to the suggested tune, think of those times when you tried doing things your way, disregarding His way. Remember how things turned out. If we can be truthful, most of us can and will quickly admit that the results weren't too great at all. In fact, in many instances, doing it our way only led to us being further behind, overwhelmed, and in a ball of confusion with much worry. Now, take another moment to think on the times when God, by His faithfulness, came through when you surrendered and gave the situation to Him! My God, my God! That deserves a shout by itself! As we keep and exercise our measure of faith, He sets things in order by His greater faith! *Keeping the Faith* is more than a song, it's a lifestyle we should all adopt!

Keeping the Faith (lyrics)

(soulful spiritual - slow tempo)

I've been there
I've been through it all

Times when I've done wrong
Times of trouble having no one to call

Times of drowning in sin
Times, for food, I had to beg and crawl

Times of hopelessness,
having no one to catch my fall

Through it all, I kept my faith in You,
though I wasn't living right
Not doing what You called me to do,
yet, You stood by me in the fight
You've always been
a constant friend indeed
so, I thank You for Your faithfulness
and all You are to me

That's why I'm keeping the faith
[keep-ing the faith]
Whoa! Yes, I'm keeping the faith
[keep-ing the faith]

It's me trusting You

with all I have and who I am;
caring for me beyond measure,
even when I get no love from them

I'm keeping the faith
in the one who is dependable and true
I'm keeping the faith
in the magnificent You!

I appreciate where I am
with testimonies from my past

Times of stumbling
Times of living life coming up last

Times of pleasing me first
and always placing You last
You still had mercy on this fool
and delivered me whenever I asked

Through it all, I kept my faith in You,
though I wasn't living right
Not doing what You called me to do,
yet, You stood by me in the fight
You've always been
a constant friend indeed
so, I thank You for Your faithfulness
and all You are to me

That's why I'm keeping the faith
[keep-ing the faith]
Whoa! Yes, I'm keeping the faith
[keep-ing the faith]

It's me trusting You
with all I have and who I am;
caring for me beyond measure,

even when I get 66no love from them

I'm keeping the faith
in the one who is dependable and true
I'm keeping the faith
in the magnificent You!

My God! My Jesus!
It's by Your Holy Spirit,
I'm keeping the faith!

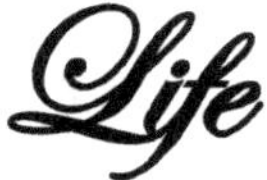

Life is a song written with the intent of taking us on a reflective, appreciative journey. The lyrics serve to honor the family structure as designed by God. It blends well with a mellow (smooth) tempo melody. It's a thoughtful happy song meant for resting our minds and hearts in joy for the simplicity of each role within the family. It showcases how each person plays an intricate part in inspiring a life worth living. The song also reminds us how significant each person's role and responsibility is. Above all, *Life* illustrates how we are created beings brought forth to do life with a great and gracious God!

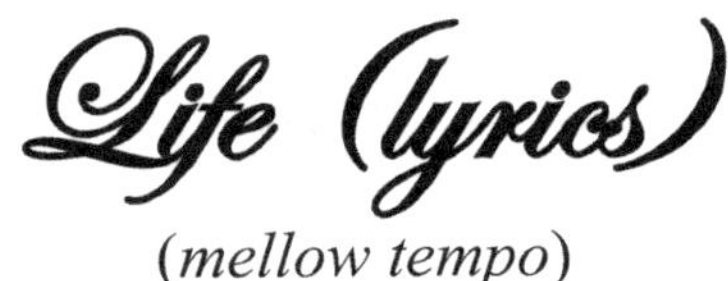

Life (lyrics)

(*mellow tempo*)

Life as a husband
is my calling to be
Protecting all under my umbrella,
responsible for my family

Life is good, it is great!
Thank You, Lord, for this fate!

Life as a father
matured me to be who I am,
learning how to lead
by serving the least of them

Life is good, it is great!
Thank You, Lord, for this fate!

Life as a wife
is my calling to be
A partner alongside my husband,
chosen by Your favor towards me

Life is good, it is great!
Thank You, Lord, for this fate!

Life as a mother
blessed with children to teach
Sharing godly love in this world,

well beyond my reach

Life is good, it is great!
Thank You, Lord, for this fate!

Life, Life
Oh, how blessed we are…
Many take it for granted
because they don't understand it
It's when we accept our positions
as designed by You
that we can begin living abundant lives
according to Your word of truth

Life as a son
as I was born to be
Growing from a boy to a man,
blessed with a father to guide me

Life is good, it is great!
Thank You, Lord, for this fate!

Life as a daughter
and very proud to be
Full of compassion and dreams,
blessed with a mother to guide me

Life is good, it is great!
Thank You, Lord, for this fate!

Life, Life
Oh, how blessed we are…
Many take it for granted
because they don't understand it
It's when we accept our positions
as designed by You
that we can begin living abundant lives

according to Your word of truth

Life as a friend
is what I have in You (Lord)
Forever holding me tightly,
always my breakthrough

Life is God, life is wonderful!
Thank You for being present every step of the way
You have shown Your love for us as an example
to help us live life the right way!

Maker

The lyrics of *Maker* portray the origination, deterioration, and redemption journey of the relationship between God and man. The lyrics are written for a mellow tempo melody. Although the context takes a historical view, the pattern parallels our relationship condition with God today. All too often, many of us proudly call on and praise God when things are selfishly in our favor. However, when things go awry, we quickly and boldly are quick to point the finger at God for "not being there" or "not intervening".

What *Maker* does is focuses on the undying and unconditional love of God initiated and demonstrated towards us. By Him being the Maker, we are His craftsmanship and with that being the case, there are times when adjustments and tune-ups are required to keep us functioning within our individual purpose. This song serves as an eye-opener for drawing us closer to God by recognizing and accepting His constant grace and love rather than condemning and distancing ourselves from God because of our shortcomings. It's a reminder that God [the *Maker*] is in the reconciling business for our best interest.

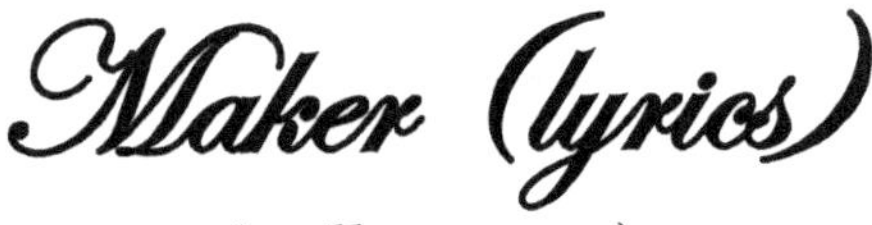

Maker (lyrics)

(mellow tempo)

You looked out into nothing
and saw me
You gathered the dust from the ground
and formed me
Into my nostrils You breathed the breath of life
in me
During the coolness of the day,
You walked beside me
Oh, how pleasant things were…

We were closer
than we've ever been
There was no separation
caused by sin
I wish now for things to be like
back then
Perfect days and
calm winds
You'd given me the world,
over a billion plus acres,
You were more than my God
You were my Maker

You saw my lack and sorrow
and made for me
a mate from the very rib
inside of me
Forever as one was Your plan

for her and me
As I was to You
was she to be to me
Oh, how pleasant things were…

Sadly, we got off track
of the plan to be
Heeded the voice of another
that came very subtly
Became shame of ourselves
by what our eyes could see
Started hiding from You
behind every bush and tree
Oh, how sad things had become…

When we came out from hiding
You provided to cover our shame
So overcome by sin
I pointed to You and her as the blame
Although there was a divide in place
You yourself became the sacrifice
Because of Your undeniable love,
for us to live You gave Your son's life
Oh, how great things had become…

We are now closer
than we've ever been
as You bridged the gap
created by sin
No longer living like I did
back then
Sweeter days ahead
as Your voice whispers in the wind
I welcome eternal life
to be spent with You later
You are more than my God
You were my Maker…

Naked and Brave

The premise of *Naked and Brave* is to stimulate courage for approaching God, regardless of our feelings of how terrible of a human being we may be or how terrible things are going for us. The lyrics are arranged for accompanying a slow tempo melody as a worship song. The focus is on us being open and true to and about ourselves before God with the understanding He isn't there to condemn us but to be the needed adjustment in our lives. The song allows for us to recognize and accept God's goodness, ask for His mercy, and receive His grace.

Sin is something we all identify with because the fact of the matter is that we are all sinners. What sets us apart as God's children is coming to the knowledge of forgiveness and accepting a right standing with God through Jesus. As we accept the truth about God being for our good, we can then be on the right track for allowing Him to perform the necessary transformational operation in our hearts and lives as we surrender to Him *Naked and Brave*. Each day of God's Holy Spirit and word operating in our lives brings about changes, resulting in a lifestyle of godly character with less practicing of sin. It's an awesome conversion which releases a huge burden of carrying and performing vain works. Here's what Jesus says in Matthew 11:28-30, "Take my yoke upon you, and learn from me; for I am gentle and lowly in heart, and you will find rest for your souls. For my yoke is easy, and my burden is light." Make it a point to remain *Naked and Brave* as you continually walk with the Lord!

Naked and Brave (lyrics)

(worship – slow tempo)

I found mercy and grace
when I acknowledged all my flaws,
from living and being unforgiving,
breaking many of Your laws
Thinking I could serve You,
all the while doing wrong
Living the life of the streets
and on Sundays singing church songs

In my soul I sensed something wasn't right
Jesus didn't die for me to live that type of life
(pause)
I called out to You
for changing me from who I was
(pause)
You then said unto me
to accept Your love

It was then I began to look to the cross
to be saved
as I cried and surrendered to You
I realized I was naked and brave

You never change who You are,
rightfully so because You are God
The change begins with us
inviting You into our hearts

We must understand that
You are not someone whom we should be afraid
You provide the godly inspiration
for us to come before You naked and brave

Because of Your mercy and grace
I'm now able to overcome my past
I now live to represent You
in the midst of a worldly cast
I have strong confidence in serving You,
following the path paved
All made possible by Jesus
when He died and rose from the grave
There's no longer any shame
standing before You naked and brave

In my soul I now know what's right
Jesus died for me to live a better life
(pause)
I thank You for making me
who I am today
(pause)
You took all my sins
and cast them far away

I will forever remember the cross
and You rising from the grave
as I lift my hands on bended knees
thanking You as I am, naked and brave

You never change who You are,
rightfully so because You are God
The change begins with us
inviting You into our hearts
We must understand that
You are not someone whom we should be afraid

You provide the godly inspiration
for us to come before You naked and brave

Naked and brave
is the beginning of salvation
Naked and brave
brings us to heaven's celebration
Naked and brave
is our goodbye to worldly things
Naked and brave
as we stand before the King of Kings

Of Love Unto Salvation

Of Love Unto Salvation is a personal favorite for me due to the fact of it being a song that promotes release. The lyrics are written to complement a country tone with an up-tempo melody. Each stanza poses an intriguing question from a person who sees negativity as being bigger than God. The target person is one who exhibits peace and joy because of their full trust in God – always seeing God bigger than anything. The answer to each of the questions posed drills down to God loving us unto salvation as the reason for not giving attention to negativity and instead, giving glory to God.

All too often we get trapped in the hustle and bustle of the day to the point of self-inflicting unnecessary stresses and illnesses which detrimentally affect our health, strength, and spiritual life. As Christians, what kind of example is it for the world to see us being defeated by worries and stresses? Too often we harbor and glorify resentments, worries, and anxieties without realizing all they are doing is blurring our vision of God. However, if we can take a breather and put faith in action by trusting God as much as we pray to Him, I believe we will have happy, contagious, and more enjoyable lives to live. Be encouraged by holding onto *Of Love Unto Salvation.*

Of Love Unto Salvation (lyrics)

(*Country tone - up-tempo*)

Hey!
What are you so happy about?
Don't you see all that's going on
in the world around?

There's killing, protesting,
inequalities, everyone's on edge,
no one's on even ground

Hey!
Why are you being so kind?
I know there's a catch
for you being that way

No one does anything
without expecting something
It's the hypocritical heart of today

Hey!
Why don't you answer me?
What is it you are taking
that makes you so calm yet blind?

Tell or show me what it is

so I can take the same trip as you
for relieving my mind

He responded, “I have
a hope beyond what is seen
I know there’s more to life
than focusing on things
I have an upbeat in my soul,
given by the One who holds
the universe in His hands,
something many don’t understand
Having His love is a celebration
and to top it off, I have salvation!

I have love unto salvation,
love unto salvation,
love unto salvation,
love unto sal-va-tion”

Hey!
That sounds good and such
but how does it measure up
to all that’s going on?

There’s too much needing to be fixed,
no time for being high
and relishing in religious fun

Hey!
If what you have is truly real,
how is it the answer
for correcting all that’s wrong?

I don’t have time
to hear a lot of preaching
so please don’t take long

He responded, “I know of the troubles
many face in this world
everyone wants the gold and diamonds
no one wants the wisdom pearl
We must realize that peace only comes
from what is greater
which only comes by repentance,
surrender and acceptance of the Savior!”

And then he went on to say, “I have
a hope beyond what is seen
I know there’s more to life
than focusing on things
I have an upbeat in my soul,
given by the One who holds
the universe in His hands,
something many don’t understand
Having His love is a celebration
and to top it off, I have salvation!

He provides love unto salvation,
love unto salvation,
love unto salvation,
love unto sal-va-tion”

Patching Up The Past

Patching Up The Past is written as a personal song that relates to many through a few common failures experienced in life which produced voids needing to be filled. The lyrics are designed to accompany a slow tempo melody as they trace unpleasant, vulnerable and memorable periods of our lives. The chorus provides the shake we need to be brought back to the reality of truth – Jesus is in the patch work business!

Whether we've been walking with God for a few seconds or a majority of our lives, none of us are exempt from life's pitfalls that will surely shake us and test our faith. What *Patching Up the Past* does is remind us that Jesus is the same yesterday, today, and forever (Hebrews 13:8). Knowing this should give us the confidence needed that, "This too shall pass". As we constantly read and partake of the Word of God, allowing it to speak to our hearts and souls, we become strengthened in faith and reliant on God to patch up the holes left by life's heartbreaks.

Patching Up The Past (lyrics)

(slow tempo)

I've been brokenhearted
in relationships throughout my life
Used and abused,
accepting other's wrong for right
The path I've walked
was sometimes lonely and full of pain
but I still held on
in Jesus' name

I've been fired from a good job
by no fault of my own
Left empty-handed on the streets,
having no place to call home
This journey of mine
hasn't been easy at all
But I always found peace
in Jesus' name when I call

My life has been a quilt
of many patterns and many stories,
worn, torn and restitched
yet still worth living to His glory
Sometimes I'd live life too slow
and sometimes so very, very fast
but it's the redeeming blood of Jesus
that patches up my past

Good times come but don't last always
We spend most of our lives riding the waves
trying to find a permanent high too fast

All we really need is to be humble and submit,
invite Jesus into our hearts as the perfect fit
His love fills every hole that patches up the past

I've been prejudged
by those not knowing much about me
Never given a chance to defend
against allegations made falsely
Accusations that were spoken
hit my heart to the very core
leaving me with terrible thoughts
wondering if I could take much more

What mattered most
and brought me through
were the words spoken at church
that I remember from my youth
"Know that you're never alone
and Jesus is your friend indeed!"
I know without any doubt
He not only meets, He is my need

My life has been a quilt
of many patterns and many stories,
worn, torn and restitched
yet still worth living to His glory
Sometimes I'd live life too slow
and sometimes so very, very, very fast
but it's the redeeming blood of Jesus
that patches up my past

Good times come but don't last always
We spend most of our lives riding the waves

trying to find a permanent high too fast

All we really need is to be humble and submit,
invite Jesus into our hearts as the perfect fit
His love fills every hole that patches up the past

Whatever the hole is in our life
Let Him fill it!
Let Him be peace…
Let Him be love…
Let Him be joy…
Let Him be patience…
Let Him fill in the holes with what you need!

Good times come but don't last always
We spend most of our lives riding the waves
trying to find a permanent high too fast

All we really need is to be humble and submit,
invite Jesus into our hearts as the perfect fit
His love fills every hole that patches up the past

Questions to Ask

All too often, we do to God what we do to those around us – TALK TOO MUCH WITHOUT SAYING A THING! The same can be said about the types of questions we ask. The lyrics of *Questions to Ask* provide an overview of how we unconsciously and as a priority seek answers without consideration for having a relationship. This is written as a worship slow tempo song which presses us to reverently ask the right questions.

I must humbly admit there have been and will continue to be times that I ask questions concerning what has already been answered. If I had been doing more reading and/or listening and less asking, I would have grasped the answer and asked more intelligent questions, if needed. Haphazardly asking questions is a general flaw we all share at some point in our maturing. It's not to say that asking questions is something we shouldn't do. It's to shed light on grasping what is said or read, internalizing and analyzing properly, in order to respond with a more intelligent question.

Many of us quickly and routinely cry out to God with the many "why's" of what we're experiencing in life with little reverence for who He is and without maintaining a relationship with Him. There's no time for going to church, no time for reading the Bible, no time to be held spiritually accountable, but, yet our questions are now to be His priority for answering. If we're going to ask any questions of God, be mindful of the chorus in *Questions to Ask* and proceed humbly and with caution.

Questions to Ask (lyrics)

(*worship – slow tempo*)

Everyone seems to have an answer
for everything
no one wants to admit
they know nothing
Having a lot to say
but never wanting to pray
forgetting the grace of God
given to them each and every day

Less speaking and more time listening
much can be learned
much can be learned

In our learning,
we come to know the facts
The truth humbles us
with the right questions to ask,
How do I repent?
How am I forgiven?
How do I accept Jesus in my life?
How do I start a new life for livin'?
These are questions needing
to be answered and put into action
for expanding the kingdom of God,
giving the enemy no glory or satisfaction

Let's start with the right questions to ask

Right questions
Right questions
Let's start with the right questions to ask

We've been talking far too much,
widening the gap of emptiness
doing the work of the enemy
forsaking kingdom's business
Lord, please hear our cry to You
Help us to know and walk in Your truth
Position us to hear Your voice
as we surrender all to You

less speaking and more time listening
much can be learned
much can be learned

in our learning
we come to know the facts
the truth humbles us
with the right questions to ask,
How do I repent?
How am I forgiven?
How do I accept Jesus in my life?
How do I start a new life for livin'?
These are questions needing
to be answered and put into action
for expanding the kingdom of God,
giving the enemy no glory or satisfaction

Let's start with the right questions to ask
Right questions
Right questions
Let's start with the right questions to ask

The words You speak are life
What You say will be, it will be

The words You speak are life
What You say will be, it will be
it will be, it will be, it will be,
it will be, it will be, it will be!

in our learning
we come to know the facts
the truth humbles us
with the right questions to ask,
How do I repent?
How am I forgiven?
How do I accept Jesus in my life?
How do I start a new life for living?
These are questions needing
to be answered and put into action
for expanding the kingdom of God,
giving the enemy no glory or satisfaction

Let's start with the right questions to ask…

Ready for Church

Ready for Church is intended to be a song expressing enthusiasm for being the Church and being a part of a church. It's a song written to incite a readiness in believers to collectively assemble in physical, brick and mortar meeting places to honor, praise, and worship God on one accord. The lyrics are penned to an up-tempo enrapturing melody. They provide hope in the company of likeminded believers which refuels us with much-needed, unbelievable encouragement for dealing with the world outside the church.

Growing up, many of us (when we were children) could relate to not being ready for church because (in most cases) it impeded on "our" day of rest and doing what we wanted to do over the weekend. However, as we've gotten older and matured in our walk and relationship with God, no longer does hearing "Are you ready for church?" early on a Sunday morning churn our stomachs; instead, it stirs our souls. There's a new excitement for the Lord, His word, and being among the family of believers – seeing that regardless of all that is wrong in the world and within our individual lives, God is yet greater! Together, we praise and worship our way out of those troubles and receive reassurance of God still being on the throne as we faithfully remain *Ready for Church*!

Ready for Church (lyrics)

(up-tempo)

ARE YOU READY?
READY FOR CHURCH?
Time to spend worshipping God,
with my brothers and sisters,
calling on His holy name

Yes, I'm ready!
Ready for church!
Coming together with my family,
on one accord, praising Him
Who reigns

It's the one place
to find healing from the past
for the soul, heart, and mind
while preparing you for the future
all at the same time

ARE YOU READY?
READY FOR CHURCH?
Let's give time to the Lord
which He's surely due
having died for fallible folk
like me and you

Yes, I'm ready!
Ready for church!

Getting that good word
that feeds my hungry soul
Living messages
always new, never old

It's the one place
to experience the
love of Jesus Christ,
which cleanses all manner of sin
and births us into new life

Church is that place
filled with the sinners, sick, and broken,
who are and were lost
Everyone is welcomed
Everyone is eligible for redemption
because Jesus paid the cost

Jesus makes us ready…
Jesus makes us ready…
Know that you're ready…
Know that you're ready…

ARE YOU READY?
READY FOR CHURCH?

ARE YOU READY?
READY FOR CHURCH?

Hallelujah!

ARE YOU READY?
READY FOR CHURCH?

Yes, I am, indeed I am!

ARE YOU READY?

READY FOR CHURCH?

ARE YOU READY?
READY FOR CHURCH?
The Lord is waiting there
with wide-open arms
Will you meet Him while you can?

Yes, I'm ready!
Ready for church!
My savior is waiting patiently,
not willing that any should perish,
ready to reconnect God and man

YES, I AM READY!
READY FOR CHURCH!

I hope to see you there…

Saved, Not Soft

Although the lyrics are written to accompany a slow tempo melody, *Saved, Not Soft* serves as an inspirational reminder of the strength we have in Christ. While the lyrical stanzas focus on the states of defeat we find ourselves experiencing, the lyrical chorus encourages us by clarifying 1 John 4:4, "You are of God, little children, and have overcome them, because He who is in you is greater than he who is in the world."

The enemy is forever about his job of killing, stealing, and destroying and there is no sign of him slowing to give anyone a break. It's his nature of being who he is. Knowing that he's about his business of releasing unrelentless attacks against us does not give reason for us to shrink back and throw in the towel. Instead, we are to remember that we're saved and are now employed in the army of the Lord! As soldiers, we cannot afford to be cowards who fearfully represent a mighty God. As we get into His Word, His Word becomes sowed within us to be used as a weapon when necessary. We must be very familiar with our God-issued weaponry and know when and how to use it accordingly. In doing so, our stand against the enemy will be illustrated as *Saved, Not Soft*!

Saved, Not Soft (lyrics)

(*slow tempo*)

There's a battle raging for our souls
The enemy is loaded with every imaginable weapon,
readying to take us down

He's marching forward with his army,
seeking to destroy all humanity
until there's none to be found

He has allegations
that are true and we're all guilty of
Our only defense is declaring
that we've been washed in the Messiah's blood

By His Word
we have hope
even when we're pummeled
against the ropes
We declare (we declare),

There are days we get knocked down
and are feeling rather off
Maintain your strength of faith to fight,
knowing you're saved, not soft
As long as you have hands and knees
you have a winning chance against loss
The enemy is forever defeated
because you're saved, not soft

When the enemy tirelessly comes our way
with troubles and heartaches
that appear unbearable

We must remember that the fight isn't ours
as we cry out to God in prayer,
rest in Him revealing the miracle

By His word
we have hope
even when we're pummeled
against the ropes
We declare (we declare),

There are days we get knocked down
and are feeling rather off
Maintain your strength of faith to fight,
knowing you're saved, not soft
As long as you have hands and knees
you have a winning chance against loss
The enemy is forever defeated
because you're saved, not soft

When we are awake
we can clearly see Who's standing with us
We have the Almighty's angels
protecting the ones He created and loves
His strength is placed in surrendered hands of praise
and the prayers prayed on bended knees
It's then we're reminded that Christ has already
died and rose, defeating every enemy
We can turn all fear off,
knowing we're saved, not soft
He's in control
Rest assured He's paid the ultimate cost
for us being saved, not soft

We can stand bold

By His word
we have hope
even when we're pummeled
against the ropes
We declare (we declare),

There are days we get knocked down
and are feeling rather off
Maintain your strength of faith to fight,
knowing you're saved, not soft
As long as you have hands and knees
you have a winning chance against loss
The enemy is forever defeated
because you're saved, not soft

We're saved, not soft
No longer living as the lost
All chains we cast off
We're saved, not soft!

Tailor-made Journey

Tailor-made Journey is a song that puts life into perspective. Set to a mellow tempo melody, the lyrics reveal how we're uniquely built for each of our individual journeys through life. The chorus reaffirms God's constant presence, love, and compassion through life journeys.

Oftentimes, along the way of living life, we come to a point where it seems no present help can be found, we feel alone and that others don't understand or are unable to help. It's in those times we're to open our eyes for seeking and seeing God. Those type moments are what God designs as tailor-made for getting our attention and for nurturing a relationship with Him. He knows how we [as human beings] can get so wrapped up and dependent on crediting others for our successes, help, breakthroughs, etc. There is nothing wrong with any of that but what it could (and oftentimes does) lead to is our trust in man rather than in God. That's when God intermittently steps in to give us a reality check of His involvement and a reminder to us of Him being God. He doesn't want, nor should we put, our absolute faith in any person but Him. Why? Because He's faithful! Also, because He knows that our fully trusting man is a setup for strife and division when that person is unable to come through on our behalf. God knows how the enemy will use that information to destroy relationships and discredit someone's character and/or heart. God steps in with a *Tailor-made Journey* that leads us to trusting Him and alleviating discord.

Tailor-made Journey (lyrics)

(mellow tempo)

There are many days
when things aren't going so well
People around being fickle,
if I confide in them, they're likely to bail
So many things I just keep to myself,
not wanting to burden anyone else
but there comes the time that I must release
in order for me to find some inkling of peace

That's when it becomes known
and clear
that You are near

That's when the word
You speak
touches my heart

It reaffirms that You'll never leave me
as You guide me through this tailor-made journey
You'll never put more on me than I can bear

You are the strength that I need
as You walk me through this tailor-made journey
Your limitless faithfulness is how much you care
[for me]

Things I've brought on myself

are nothing I'm proud of
But I'm sure glad that none of it
has ever hindered Your undying love
Life being life when anything happens
always interrupts the plans I'm mapping,
putting what I think best to the side
only to rely more on You as my guide

That's when it becomes known
and clear
that You are near

That's when the word
You speak
touches my heart

It reaffirms that You'll never leave me
as You guide me through this tailor-made journey
You'll never put more on me than I can bear

You are the strength that I need
as You walk me through this tailor-made journey
Your limitless faithfulness is how much you care
[for me]

My lot in life
is not what I'd hoped it to be,
so far from what I desired;
but the more I find and depend on You
the less of me remains
after being purged by life's fire

That's when it becomes known
and clear
that You are near

That's when the word

You speak
touches my heart

It reaffirms that You'll never leave me
as You guide me through this tailor-made journey
You'll never put more on me than I can bear

You are the strength that I need
as You walk me through this tailor-made journey
Your limitless faithfulness is how much you care
[for me]

Ubiquitous Influence

Ubiquitous Influence is an unrhymed worship song written to accompany a slow tempo melody. It lyrically illustrates how God's DNA is stamped within everything created. It's a song designed to graft within us thought provoking recognition of just how great God is, with glimpses of Him being ever present about us. In doing so, we allow His goodness to saturate within our very being, drawing us to pure worship.

God's presence alone promotes and provides the fruit of the Spirit (i.e., love, joy, peace, patience, kindness, goodness, faith, meekness, and temperance) for all to partake of and share with others. Such fruit can be realized upon us taking a moment of rest to reflect on Him by way of our observations, and/or interactions with living beings, animals, nature, and the universe. Comfort will be found knowing the essence of His character expands throughout all creation. When we accept the *Ubiquitous Influence* of who He is we can begin to experience complete satisfaction of who and whose we are!

Ubiquitous Influence (lyrics)

(slow tempo worship)

The entire universe,
You created
Your thoughts came alive

The sun in the day,
You created
The father lighting the universe's path

The moon in the night,
You created
The Son our hope in the darkest of times

The stars in the sky,
You created
You spoke on the sky's canvas

Humanity,
You created
We're all images of You

The air we breathe,
You created
You're the breath of life

Hearing, smelling, tasting,
seeing, touching,
You created
Senses we can use to connect with You

The love we share,
You created
It is Who You are

The talents we have,
You created
Miens of what You can do

Nature and animals,
You created
Your joy given to us

The need for mercy and grace,
You created
Calling us unto you

The plan of redemption,
You created
Sacrificing Your only Son

Reconciling us whom
You created
To be Your children forever

Heaven,
You created
Your dwelling place on high

Your DNA is everywhere
and on all creation
from the dust of earth
to every constellation
You influence the being of all…
You are the beginning of it all…
You are responsible for all…
You are ALL!!!

Veering Off Course

Veering Off Course is lyrically written as a worship song to accompany a slow tempo melody. The lyrics share a story with relatable details of how a person can think he or she is in right standing with God by being heavenly-minded but senselessly living an opposing lifestyle. It reveals how the center of glory is vain self. Oh, how we easily and often buy into the false notion of being "blessed" as living life on our own terms.

Interestingly, God will permit us to continue down such a path but will always provide eye-opening moments to get our attention, position and steer us on the track He's lain for us. Sadly, as we live life *Veering Off Course*, we find ourselves at our rope's end which God uses as a wake-up call. In that season, an opportunity is presented for us to make the best decision we could ever make – surrendering self and limited knowledge of God in exchange for Jesus and a relationship with God!

Veering Off Course (lyrics)

(worship – slow tempo)

The worst that could happen
did so
I found myself falling away
drifting slow
Thought I was strong in the Lord
Who I really didn't know
A labeled "Christian"
performing a sinner's show

My life was mine to live
and that I did on my own
Thinking I was walking with God
not realizing my sin was on the throne
I needed help from someone, somewhere
other than the contacts on my phone
I was fed up with being in a place
of darkness and feeling so all alone

I had gone too far,
felt like I was left in a desert land
No oasis on the horizon
just extreme heat beating down upon this man

I was in a place where I didn't want to be
but where I was needing to be
because it was there when I was
brought down on bended knee

As I looked to the sky, I started to confess
about how my life had become a complete mess

I really needed God to hear and heal me
was my cry and prayer with deep remorse
taking full responsibility for leaving Him
with my soul and mind veering off course
I need God
I need the Savior
I need saving from veering off course

I poured out to Him He poured into me,
making clear the error of my ways
A fresh new start I was given,
accepting His cost paid for me to be saved
I began relying on His Holy Spirit
to keep me in His arms to stay
so that my eternal future will be with Him
filled with glorious days

Being in a better place in life
than where I was before,
showed the power of His love
to close those dangerous doors
Having Him in my heart
only leads to me wanting Him more
He delivered me from so much sin
and gave me something worth living for

I had gone too far,
felt like I was left in a desert land
No oasis on the horizon
just extreme heat beating down upon this man

I was in a place where I didn't want to be
but where I was needing to be

because it was there when I was
brought down on bended knee

As I looked to the sky, I started to confess
how my life had become a complete mess

I really needed God to hear and heal me
as I cried and prayed with deep remorse
taking full responsibility for leaving Him
with my soul and mind veering off course
I need God
I need the Savior
I need saving from veering off course

Your way is the path to follow,
which I will walk everyday,
forgetting all the sin behind me
as You lead me along Your way
No longer will I be subject
to living life by any fleshly force
I now have the Almighty within me
to keep me from veering off course!
I need God
I need the Savior
I need saving from veering off course…

Where I'm Going From Here

Where I'm Going From Here is written as a worship song set to a slow tempo melody along with background singers or a choir echoing the lyrics within brackets and joining the main vocalist during the chorus. The song is meant to encourage the soul beyond the sorrows of life. It reminds us of the security and faith we have in God as well as having His promise of the Holy Spirit living within us. Regardless of where we came from or are going through, the future God has prepared for us is so much greater. We must not only accept it [God's plan] as it is sown in our hearts but feed it by the word of God so that it consumes our entire being.

As we personally and individually realize *Where I'm Going From Here* rests in our confidence in God, we can then deliver spontaneous praise and worship to God!

Where I'm Going From Here (lyrics)

(*worship – slow tempo*)

Everyone has a past
What matters is the present
[Do you know what you're doing?]
[Do you know where you're going?]

Many wish this life would last
Many have lives unpleasant
[Do you know what you're doing?]
[Do you know where you're going?]

Let today be the day
that you surrender

Don't rest in delay
from sharing in His eternal splendor

Yesterday can't be changed
No need of tormenting yourself
[Do you know what you're doing?]
[Do you know where you're going?]

He's able to break those chains
He's calling you to Himself
[Do you know what you're doing?]

[Do you know where you're going?]

Let today be the day
that you surrender

Don't rest in delay
from sharing in His eternal splendor…

The Holy Spirit is ready to take the lead
God has better in store for you
Jesus has forgiven and washed your past
The Father will make all things new
There's no load too heavy for Him to carry
There's no reason for you to fear
He's ready to receive you as you are
He has better in store for you from here

Living without a future is vain
There are greater opportunities ahead
[Do you know what you're doing?]
[Do you know where you're going?]

Let go of the pride and shame
Grab hold of His scarlet thread
[Do you know what you're doing?]
[Do you know where you're going?]

Let today be the day
that you surrender

Don't rest in delay
from sharing in His eternal splendor

He's reaching out to you
He's offering an eternity of blessedness
[Do you know what you're doing?]
[Do you know where you're going?]

This journey you're on, He'll bring you through,
bestowing on you a life of preciousness
[Do you know what you're doing?]
[Do you know where you're going?]

Let today be the day
that you surrender

Don't rest in delay
from sharing in His eternal splendor...

The Holy Spirit is ready to take the lead
God has better in store for you
Jesus has forgiven and washed your past
The Father will make all things new
There's no load too heavy for Him to carry
There's no reason for you to fear
He's ready to receive you as you are
He has better in store for you from here

Know Him,
Trust Him,
Love Him,
He has a future for you

Know Him,
Trust him,
Love Him,
He has a future for you...

The Holy Spirit is ready to take the lead
God has better in store for you
Jesus has forgiven and washed your past
The Father will make all things new
There's no load too heavy for Him to carry
There's no reason for you to fear

He’s ready to receive you as you are
He has better in store for you from here

He is your future!

Xeroxed

Xeroxed is lyrically written to accompany a mellow tempo melody. It serves as a revival song for awakening us from the hypnosis of the world to the reality of being new creations in Christ. As new creations, we are branded as Christians and replicas of Jesus. It becomes evident in our lifestyles (i.e., how we live, the things we say, etc.) as we reciprocate the blessing of God with sincere and willful intent.

If we're being honest with ourselves, we can all admit that we've been comfortable as carbon copies of this world far too long and, in most cases, much longer than replicas of Christ. Yes, we stand bold in declaring our faith and proclamations of being Christians but, sadly, many of us have been living contradictory lifestyles. It's past time that we examine what is written in our hearts (that which inspires and guides our living) and see if it lines up with what's in God's Word (i.e., the Bible). The more we read and partake of the correct teachings of God, the more we're apt to become *Xeroxed* productions of Jesus. By no means is it a fast-paced, quick-fix, pain-free action. It's a lifetime of adjustments and development which not only benefits us individually but becomes intertwined with our purpose for serving those around us.

Let what the world witnesses and sees in and about you be the *Xeroxed* word of God manifested in the words and deeds of your life.

Xeroxed (lyrics)

(mellow *tempo*)

My life has changed,
it seems like in a blink of an eye
Although it didn't happen that fast,
the old me is behind and that's no lie

The original me
was filled with weights and sins
holding me down
That's why I needed Jesus in my life
to turn things around

When I answered His calling,
my eyes were opened
as tears ran down my face
I was overwhelmed by
His amazing grace

No longer am I living for myself
trying to find what the world can't offer
I had to close the book on ghostwriters
and return to the original Author
That's when I received
what I've been searching after,
a life that was xeroxed for me
from the heart of the Master!

A copy of this world, I am no longer

I'm now an original
xeroxed from the heart of the Master

Now I have an unspeakable joy
which I can't explain
No reason to give a reason
but I will share how you can get the same

Be true to yourself
and know that what you're looking for
in this world can't be found
Release your heart to God
and bask in His glorious sound

[saying]

"You are loved, you are forgiven,
you are being built upon Jesus the Rock!

Your search is over
You're a new exposure

No longer this world's carbon copy,
from my heart you've been xeroxed"

No longer do you live for yourself
trying to find what the world can't offer
You had to close the book on ghostwriters
and return to the original Author
That's when you received
what you've been searching after,
a life that was xeroxed for you
from the heart of the Master!

A copy of this world, you are no longer
You're now an original in this world
xeroxed from the heart of the Master

There's no one quite like you
You've been reborn brand new

When people see you
they see an image of God, too

You are unique and wonderfully made
with a bright future ahead as yesterday fades

You're being rebuilt upon the Rock,
straight from the heart of God, xeroxed

No longer do you live for yourself
trying to find what the world can't offer
You had to close the book on ghostwriters
and return to the original Author
That's when you received
what you've been searching after,
a life that was xeroxed for you
from the heart of the Master!

You Have All You Need

You Have All You Need is written as a dialogue between a non-believer and a believer. It is set to a slow tempo melody and is meant to showcase the peace that can only be found in God, regardless of the appearance and goings on of all else around.

When you've been walking with the Lord for a while, you eventually come to a point where the things of yesterday no longer affect your attitude, mind, health, and responses today. Part of it is simply because not only are you secure in knowing who and Whose you are, but you've grown into realizing that *You Have All You Need*. Whenever we come to a place in our faith and development where we accept and trust God as being all we need, our perspective about everything changes (for the good). We no longer fight against every fiery dart that comes our way. We become more strategic and confident in God's ability and protection. We no longer find and place value in what we have (be it the apparel, jewelry, vehicles, bank account size, etc.) but in Who has us. When we arrive at the restful state of God being all we need, we have total peace and can be always content in all things. Spending time with God and forging a relationship with Him produces *You Have All You Need*!

You Have All You Need (lyrics)

(*slow tempo*)

Looking at you,
things don't appear so great
Seeing the lack in your life
is not an enviable fate

PERCEPTION IS JUST THAT,
NO ONE KNOWS FOR CERTAIN YOUR STORY!

YET, YOU SEEM AT PEACE
IN THE MIDST OF A BROWBEATEN QUARRY!

Where do you find strength for the day?
Who is it that you turn to for help?
Why do you not count yourself out?
What's your plan for the next step?

Is there something wrong with you?
You don't seem to get what I'm saying
I'm trying to reach out to you best I can
so, why are you committed to praying?

YOU'RE LEAVING ME NO OTHER CHOICE
BUT TO GIVE UP ON YOU!

HELP ME TO UNDERSTAND
WHATEVER IT IS YOU'RE GOING THROUGH!

Where do you find strength for the day?
Who is it that you turn to for help?
Why do you not count yourself out?
What's your plan for the next step?

You look at me as though I'm the fool
when you're the one doing without
You can't even take a stand for yourself
and you're constantly being talked about

STAND AND DEFEND YOURSELF
IF I'M WRONG BY WHAT I SAY!

STOP STANDING BY ALLOWING OTHERS
TO TREAT YOU ANY WAY!
Where do you find strength for the day?
Who is it that you turn to for help?
Why do you not count yourself out?
What's your plan for the next step?

THEN YOU SAID TO ME,
"I HAVE ALL I NEED IN JESUS...

I'm not who or what you see naturally
The riches I possess are not outside but inside of me
Don't be deceived in thinking I'm down and out
I'm pressing on in sharing the gospel throughout
My success isn't measured by the ways of the lost
My value is found in Jesus dying on the cross
The freedom I have is something this world can't provide
They count themselves free, all the while chained to pride
I have God's perfect peace, joy, and love indeed
There's nothing greater you can offer me
I present this offer for you to learn and receive the same

It takes repenting and accepting forgiveness in Jesus' name
It'll be a shame for you to pass on this free and eternal gift
He's ready to take the burden you've been carrying if
You yield your heart and life to His will
Then and only then can the void in your life be filled
Take the failproof chance and you'll see
that He's all you need!

HE'S ALL YOU NEED!
HE'S ALL YOU NEED!
HE'S ALL YOU NEED!
HE'S ALL YOU NEED!

He's all you need…"

Zealous About That Life

Z*ealous About That Life* offers an up-tempo sigh of relief in response to knowing God. This is a tune written for those who have experienced the faithfulness and goodness of God through testimonies worthy of praise! He is Who He is and so much more beyond our knowledge! This song is for showering God with the worship and praise due Him as it reminds us of a few specific attributes of His that were manifested on our behalf. He is a merciful and gracious God! The more we know of Him, walk with Him, and share Him, the more we have reason to be *Zealous About That Life*!

Zealous About That Life (lyrics)

(*up-tempo*)

What's better
than what you have?
Who's greater
than who has you?
Who's stronger
than the Almighty?
What can
hinder your breakthrough?

Lift your head and give thanks
to the Lord,
knowing He has a plan for you
Lift your hands and give thanks
to the Lord,
for the life He's given you

Show that He's the reason
you're about that life
Let the world see that
you're about that life
Be zealous
about that life

Show that He's the reason

you're about that life
Let the world see that
you're about that life
Be zealous about
that life you have with Jesus…

What's more joyful
than being free?
Who can give you
perfect peace?
Who is it
that's in total control?
What other is worthy
of your soul?

Lift your head and give thanks
to the Lord,
knowing He has a plan for you
Lift your hands and give thanks
to the Lord,
for the life He's given you

Show that He's the reason
you're about that life
Let the world see that
you're about that life
Be zealous
about that life

Clap your hands…
Do your dance…
Let them know who you know…

Clap your hands…
Do your dance…
Let them know who you know…

Lift your head and give thanks
to the Lord,
knowing He has a plan for you
Lift your hands and give thanks
to the Lord,
for the life He's given you

Show that He's the reason
you're about that life
Let the world see that
you're about that life
Be zealous
about that life

Show that He's the reason
you're about that life
Let the world see that
you're about that life
Be zealous about
that life you have with Jesus…AMEN!

In Closing

Not all songs are meant for everyone. However, everyone has a song. Songs enhance our lives whether by encouraging our souls, inspiring our purpose, comforting our tears, or motivating our calls to action. No matter how, when, where, what, or why, the occasion for having a song in the timing needed is a must for most human beings. That is why I've taken the opportunity to write this book, as a gift to share songs which comfort the heart by introducing (or reintroducing) the love of God that is so much needed today.

Oftentimes, many obliviously credit secular songs for relating to them when, in actuality, those songs keep them lingering in unpleasant states outside of their purpose. What the songs within *A Song in the Timing I Needed* do is remind everyone of the goodness of God and attempt to position each of us in a heart of worship that is everlasting and nurtures us in the ways of God. Singers and celebrities are fallible humans who can and will let us down. However, God is the same yesterday, today, and forever and He changes not! Just like vehicles use various grades of fuel for optimum performance based on the manufacturer's design, so it is with us. We need the songs and Word of God to fuel our lives for optimum performance towards our purpose as designed by the Manufacturer (GOD)!

Be encouraged, sing your song in the timing needed, and be a blessing to those around you by sharing God, who lives through you!

Author Owen Watson, Ph.D.

Read biography and get an exclusive inside look at exciting upcoming new titles

www.drowenwatson.com

Email: drowenwatson@outlook.com

BOOKS BY
Author Owen Watson, Ph.D.

It's in Their DNA: What and Why Men and Women Do Not Ask and Do Not Answer

Relentless Grace: Behind the Scenes of Men

There is Jesus: Prayers for Life's Journey

Prayers for Life's Journey

Fighting Cancer One Poem a Day (50 states & D.C. series)

Behind My Glorious Smile (by Antoinette Thomas & Owen Watson, Ph.D.)

Betting on Me: Revelatory Concepts for Success

Defeating Cancer One Poem a Day

Po' Man Ain't Got Not Much Say

What Matters Most: Family, Friends, and Foes

www.ingramcontent.com/pod-product-compliance
Lightning Source LLC
LaVergne TN
LVHW010929110826
845149LV00013B/2523

* 9 7 8 1 9 5 7 4 2 0 0 8 0 *